Mexican Christmas

COOKBOOK

JAIME IRAM VARGAS BARRIENTOS

INTRODUCTION

The classic Mexican Christmas was born from the cross between Christian celebrations and the rites of the native communities. Iconic elements such as *posadas* and *piñatas* began as a strategy to evangelize endemic populations through songs and images representing the birth of Jesus.

The use of the poinsettia (*Noche Buena*) as an ornamental plant became popular due to its seasonal flowering, and the use of turkey as the star food of the feast was only possible in the 20th century by the influence of Thanksgiving Day on the Mexican border.

Rural communities have an internal organization for the preparation of these holidays. Everything revolves around the downtown temple where the parishioners, who gather for the *posadas,* sing carols describing the journey of Joseph and Mary; money is thrown to be caught by the children, called *bolo*, and a 7-pointed *piñata* is broken to represent the sins committed during the year.

The food is important because usually more than one family participate in the preparation of *tamales*, frying the fritters or cooking the fruit for the punch. Poinsettia is used in the decoration, spheres are hung in the temple and houses, as well as nativity scenes with figures that represent characters of the Christian Advent.

The children are given bags of sweets called *aguinaldos* at the end of the *posada*, and finally *tamales* are distributed between neighbors to celebrates the community union.

The religious character of these holidays has allowed its continuity in Mexico, and the deep-rooted tradition has made it possible to enjoy the nostalgic flavors of the past.

PRESENTATION

In conversation with foreign friends, the subject of food always raises a fascination because of the differences and contrasts that exist on tables around the world. When I have mentioned the ways of cooking and eating in the Mexican cuisine, questions about certain ingredients that sound exotic or that have never been heard of before, tend to come up.

On a trip to England, I realized the difficulties involved in preparing a Mexican dish in foreign lands, no matter how simple the recipe was or how many ingredients were needed, the variety of products or instruments found that far from home were not always the best to cook the traditional dish properly.

It was only recently with the request of colleagues for Mexican Christmas recipes, that the idea of a cookbook that not only contained classic dishes, but also proposed substitutions for ingredients that are difficult to obtain, came up.

This book is a first effort to bring nostalgic flavors from Mexico to everyone's table at Christmas Eve.

¡Buen provecho!

CONTENT

Starters

December's celebrations can have different appetizers that are not necessarily exclusive to Christmas. Social parties throughout the year use creamy and spreadable preparations on tortilla chips, buns or crackers as starters.

Some of them have a long tradition on Mexican tables but, most of them have only become popular in the last century with the American influence of fancy meals for social and family gatherings at home.

Apricot Cheese Log

Ingredients

250 g cream cheese
1 cup g toasted pecan
30 g sugar

Apricot jam
300 g fresh or dried apricot
1 lemon juice
100 g sugar
2 cups water

Instructions

1.   Beat cream cheese with sugar in a large bowl until smooth. Wrap in plastic. Refrigerate at least 1 hour.
2.   Chop pecans and place in a shallow plate. Shape cheese mixture into two 6-in.-long logs; roll in pecans to coat evenly. Wrap logs and refrigerate at least 1 hour.
3.   Meanwhile, cooked the apricots in a saucepan with lemon juice, sugar and water for 20 minutes. Blend them with a food processor and let it cool.
4.   Unwrap logs and cover them with this jam to serve.

Guacamole

Ingredients

4 ripe avocados
2 tablespoons chopped coriander
1 lemon juice
½ onion
2 fresh green chilies or
3 tablespoons of chopped pickled jalapeño peppers
1 pinch salt
1 pinch black pepper

Instructions

1.   Remove the seeds of the avocados and scoop out the pulp from the peel. Mash the pulp and make a purée.
2.   Chop the tomato, onion and fresh chili into small cubes, mix with the purée, lemon juice, coriander and season with salt and pepper.

Pork Beans

Ingredients

1 kg cooked beans
½ kg lard
½ kg Mexican chorizo or pork curated meat
500 g mozzarella cheese
1 can of pickled jalapeños peppers or two fresh chilies
½ kg pork ham
50 g drained can pitted black olives

Instructions

1.   Mash the beans with a masher to make a purée.
2.   Also chop the ham, the olives, the cheese and the jalapeño.
3.   In a large saucepan place the lard and fry the chorizo in low heat. Once fried, add the beans and move constantly.
4.   Toss the chopped ingredients and stir; if you use fresh chili add a tablespoon of white vinegar.
5.   Remove from heat when thickened. Serve with corn chips.

Requesón

Ingredients

½ kg requeson or ricotta cheese
2 tomatoes
½ onion
1 garlic clove
2 green chilies
1 tablespoon oil

Instructions

1.   Diced finely the onion, garlic, chilies and tomatoes.
2.   Cook in the saucepan with the oil until tender, then add the ricotta and stir.
3.   Serve with corn chips or bread.

Pasta first appeared in the coasts of Mexico with the arrival of the European people. At the beginning, it was served as a fancy preparation for the feasts of the elite in the colonial era. The popular types were tagliatelle, macaroni, ravioli, and noodles cooked with foreign spices and served in broths with cheese.

As a social and high-class food, it endured in big celebrations such as Christmas, but until the 20th century it became a popular dish when local ingredients were incorporated into its preparations. In Christmas, it is common to serve a creamy pasta along with nuts and fruits or spiced with chili.

Chipotle Spaghetti

Ingredients

500 g dried spaghetti
400 g cream cheese
1 can chipotle peppers
60 g butter
½ onion
100 ml chicken stock
1 cup whole milk
Two spoon olive oil

Instructions

1.   Cook the pasta according to the packet instructions in a pan of boiling salted water with the onion and the oil, then drain and reserve the onion.
2.   Blend the onion with the rest of ingredients. Place the sauce in a large frying pan on a medium-high heat until thickened.
3.   Toss the drained pasta into the sauce pan, stir, taste, season and plate.

Cheese Sauce Fusilli

Ingredients

200 g cream cheese
250 g mozzarella cheese
400 g dried fusilli
2 cups sour cream
1 cup milk
1 cup chicken stock
1 spoon olive oil
60 g butter
1 onion
4 garlic cloves
100 g chopped bacon
2 spoon chopped parsley
1 pinch nutmeg

Instructions

1.   Cook the fusilli according to the packet instructions in a pan of boiling salted water with a spoon of oil, then drain it.
2.   Peel and finely chop the garlic and the onion. Melt the butter with the olive oil in a large frying pan, add the onion, garlic and bacon and cook until crispy, set aside.
3.   Blend the cream cheese, cream, mozzarella, milk, chicken stock and salt.
4.   Toss them to the bacon pan, heat until thickened.
5.   Add the drained pasta to the cheese sauce, then mix, taste, season with nutmeg and plate with the parsley.

Christmas Cold Pasta

Ingredients

200 g pecan
400 g dried pene rigatte
1/2 cups crème fraiche
2 cups Greek yogurt
60 g sugar
2 pinch salt
300 g diced ham
500 g diced canned pineapple
400 g green grape
200 g dried cranberry

Instructions

1.   Cook the rigate according to the packet instructions in a pan of boiling salted water with a spoon of oil, then drain it.
2.   Stir the crème fraiche with the yogurt, sugar and salt.
3.   Toss the rest of the ingredients with the pasta into the cream, then mix, taste, season and plate.

Codito Soup

Ingredients

500 g dried macaroni
200 g ham in cubes
2 cups sour cream
2 tablespoon mayonnaise
2 tablespoon American mustard
1 pinch pepper
2 celery stick
100 g caned pineapple slices

Instructions

1.   Cook the macaroni according to the packet instructions in a pan of boiling salted water, then drain it.
2.   Stir the cream with the mayonnaise and the mustard, season with salt and pepper.
3.   Dice the ham and chop the celery and pineapple into small pieces. Toss them with the pasta into the cream, then mix, taste, season and plate.

Poblano Spaghetti

Ingredients

400 g dried spaghetti
50 g Parmesan cheese
480 g rip poblano chili or green pepper bell
60 g butter
½ onion
50 ml chicken stock
4 heaped tablespoons crème fraîche
1 cup whole milk
1 cup sweet corn kernels
3 garlic cloves
1 spoon flour

Instructions

1.   Cook the pasta in a pan according to the packet instructions of boiling salted water, then drain.
2.   Peel and finely slice the garlic, the pepper bell and the onion. Place them in a large frying pan on a medium-high heat with the butter and the flour. Season with salt and cook for 6 minutes.
3.   Blend the mixture with crème fraîche, stock, milk and Parmesan cheese.
4.   Place the sauce in a large frying pan on a medium-high heat until thickened.
5.   Toss the drained pasta and the kernels into the cream pan, stir, taste, season and plate.

Buñuelos

A classic dessert during the holiday season are the *buñuelos* (fritters), a sweet fried dough of Spanish heritage that positioned itself as a favorite treat during winter.

Throughout all Mexican territory, fritters are eaten and prepared with some differences in the recipe and size when they are served, but it is common to eat them soaked in a spiced syrup or sprinkled with a mixture of sugar with cinnamon.

The syrup ingredients

500 g brown sugar
500 g guavas
2 cup water
1 cinnamon stick
2 cloves
1 orange peel

Instructions

1.   Boil the water with brown sugar, cloves and cinnamon until dissolved. Toss in it the orange peel and the sliced and pitted guavas. Cook until syrup thickens.

Buñuelo de Viento

Ingredients

400 g plain flour
½ teaspoon salt
4 tablespoon sugar
1 teaspoon baking powder
4 whisked eggs
½ cup water
60 g melted butter
1 cup evaporated milk
1 l vegetable oil

Instructions

1.   Mix flour, salt, sugar and baking powder in a bowl. Add the eggs, water and whisk, then pour the milk and whisk again until you have a smooth, thick batter; wrap and set aside to rest 20 minutes.
2.   Heat the oil in a wide and deep pan. Immerse the fritter mold in the oil for one minute to be heated, then take out and immediately immerse 3/4 parts of it in the batter, take it out and wait for 10 seconds, then immerse again in the oil.
3.   Wait until fritter separate from the mold, then turn it regularly with kitchen clamps until crisp and a medium brown color.
4.   Drain on kitchen paper. Let it cool briefly, then you can toss in spiced sugar.

**You can use a cookie cutter or a masher as a buñuelo mold*

Cheese Buñuelo

Ingredients

400 g plain flour
100 g ground cheese
1 teaspoon baking powder
1 beaten egg
30 g butter
2 tablespoon + 1 cup sugar
1 pinch salt
1 star anise
200 ml water
1 L vegetable oil
2 tablespoon ground cinnamon

Instructions

1.   Make an infusion with the water and the anise.
2.   Mix two tablespoon sugar, baking powder, salt and flour in a bowl. Add the egg, soft butter and cheese.
3.   Add slowly the infusion and knead all together until the dough is smooth and no sticky. As needed, add flour.
4.   Rest the dough for 20 minutes covered with a damp kitchen towel.
5.   Then divide the dough into small balls and let them rest for 15 minutes more.
6.   Take a ball of dough and roll out to a thin and transparent disc.
7.   Let rest the discs for 40 minutes over a kitchen towel.
8.   Meanwhile, mix the rest of the sugar with the cinnamon.
9.   Heat the oil in a wide and deep pan, fry the discs until crisp and a rich brown color, turning regularly.
10.   Drain on kitchen paper and toss in the spiced sugar.

Knee Buñuelo

Ingredients

1 teaspoon baking powder
½ cup warm water
2 cup plain flour
1 tablespoon butter
1 egg
½ tablespoon anise liquor
1 spoon sugar
1 L beef lard

Instructions

1.   Mix the sugar, baking powder and flour in a bowl. Add the egg, soft butter, water and liquor.
2.   Knead all together until the dough is smooth and no sticky. Let it rest for 3 hours.
3.   Divide the dough into small balls and stretch with your hands resting on your knee or the base of an upturned bowl until to a diameter of 12-15 cm. Let these discs rest for 1 hour to dry over a clean kitchen towel.
4.   Heat the beef lard in a wide and deep pan, fry the buñuelos until crisp and a medium brown color, turning regularly.
5.   Drain on kitchen paper.
6.   Serve with brown sugar syrup.

**A buñuelo disc has to be transparent enough to let the light through when placed it against the sunlight before being fried*

Mexican Beignets (sapitos)

Ingredients

750 g plain flour
750 ml milk
1 teaspoon baking powder
1 teaspoon vanilla extract
5 g yeast
1 pinch salt
1 L vegetable oil
1 tablespoon sugar
1 cup caster sugar
1 cup warm water
2 cups pastry cream

Instructions

1.   Mix the water with the yeast and the sugar, set aside to rest 15 minutes or until it gets puffy.
2.   Mix flour and baking powder in a bowl. Add the yeast and the vainilla; knead until you have a smooth dough, cover and set aside to rest.
3.   Roll out the dough on a clean surface to 5 mm thick. Cut squares with a knife.
4.   Heat the oil in a wide and deep pan; drop the squares into the oil. Using a slotted spoon, constantly turn the fritters over in the hot oil to brown and puffy. Remove and drain on kitchen paper.
5.   Cover them with caster sugar and fill them with pastry cream.

Pumpkin Buñuelo

Ingredients

1 kg plain flour
1 cup sugar
1 teaspoon baking powder
140 g lard
½ pumpkin purée can or
1 cup mashed cooked pumpkin
Water needed
1 cup pecan
1 cup maple syrup
1 L vegetable oil

Instructions

1.   Mix and knead all the first 6 ingredients. Add water as needed.
2.   Knead all together until the dough is smooth and no sticky.
3.   Divide the dough into small balls and roll out with a rolling pin until it is thin and transparent. Let these discs rest for 1 hour to dry.
4.   Heat the oil in a wide and deep pan, fry the buñuelos until crisp and a medium brown color, turning regularly.
5.   Then drain on kitchen paper.
6.   Serve with maple syrup and toasted pecan.

Sopaipillas

Ingredients

500 g plain flour
4 tablespoon sugar
½ teaspoon baking powder
½ teaspoon vanilla extract
250 g melted butter
1 pinch salt
1 L vegetable oil
2 tablespoon cinnamon powder
1 cup sugar

Instructions

1.   Mix flour, salt, sugar and baking powder in a bowl. Add the butter and the vanilla; knead until you have a smooth dough, cover and set aside to rest 20 minutes.
2.   Roll out the dough on a clean surface with a rolling pin until it is thin. Cut circles and divide them in half.
3.   Heat the oil in a wide and deep pan; the oil is hot enough when a little of the batter turns golden immediately.
4.   Drop the half-circles into the oil, making puffy, moon-shaped little fritters.
5.   Using a slotted spoon, constantly turn the fritters over in the hot oil to brown. Remove and drain on kitchen paper.
6.   Roll the fritters in a cinnamon and sugar mix.

Tamales

There's a wide variety of tamale flavors and preparations that can be found throughout the year. Even so, tamales regularly follow the same steps in all its variations.

For its elaboration it is necessary the corn husk or banana leaf, but can be substituted with greaseproof paper.

1.   Before the dough or filling preparation, soak the corn husks in a bowl of warm water until get flexible and soft.

2.   In Mexico, the corn dough is made from scratch, using corn boiled in lime water or nixtamal. It is possible to substitute with hydrated cornmeal. For the tamal batter, beat the butter and mix it with the corn dough and salt. One golden proportion is 250 – 300 g lard per corn batter kilo.

3.   When the dough and filling are ready, take a soaked corn husk or piece of greaseproof paper and spoon a heaped tablespoon of your mixture into the middle of the husk; if the husks are thin, you might have to layer two on top of each other. Fold the sides in to cover the filling, you can twist the ends and use string to tie them.

4.   Put a large pan of water on to boil; the pan needs to be big enough to fit a colander on top. Add a coin in the water, the sound of the coin moving by the boiling water indicate that is enough water inside.

5.   Lay your prepared tamales in a large colander or steamer, making sure they're all in one layer and not overlapping. Cover the top of the colander with tin foil and seal it nice and tightly. Pop the colander on top of your pan of boiling water and steam for about 40 to 45 minutes. Refilling the water when the sound of the coin stops.

Never leave the tamale pot alone, because tradition says that the tamale sits alone and gets stained or takes longer to cook.

Green Chicken Tamales

Ingredients

1 kg fine cornmeal
250 g lard
1 kg green tomatoes
10 green chilies
¼ onion
3 garlic cloves
1 cup pumpkin seed
2 skinless chicken breasts
3 heaped tablespoon salt
1 L water
1 teaspoon baking powder
20 Corn husks or greaseproof paper

Instructions

1.   Cook the chicken in a large pan of water with one clove of garlic and one tablespoon of salt.
2.   In another pan boil the tomatoes, chili and rest of the garlic. Blend it all with one cup of stock and the pumpkin seed.
3.   Chop the onion and fry in a sauce pan with one tablespoon of lard. Toss the chili sauce, taste and add salt if needed.
4.   Shred the breast chicken and toss it in the chili sauce.
5.   Prepare the corn dough, mixing the cornmeal, 4 cup of the chicken stock and the rest of the lard.
6.   Take a soaked corn husk and spoon enough corn dough into the middle of the husk; fill it with the chili chicken stew and fold the sides in to cover the mixture.
7.   Lay your prepared tamales in a large steamer, as the indications above. Steam for about 40 to 45 minutes.

Mole Tamales

Ingredients

1 kg fine cornmeal
250 g lard
1 L chicken stock
2 cooked and shredded chicken breasts
1 L mole
6 banana leaf or greaseproof paper
salt

Instructions

1.   Hydrates the cornmeal with 4 cup of chicken stock and mix with enough salt.
2.   Cream the lard in a different bowl and beat with the corn dough.
3.   Cut the banana leaf in half and into 20 cm long shape squares. Pass them quickly in the stove fire to get flexibility. Spoon enough of the corn dough into the middle of the leaf, one portion of chicken and spoonful of mole; fold the sides in to cover the mixture.
4.   Steam for about 40 to 45 minutes.

Northern Red Tamales

Ingredients

1 kg fine cornmeal
250 g beef lard
3 heaped tablespoon salt
1 fistfull of cumin seed
4 garlic cloves
1 kg pork meat
1 L water
20 pieces dried red chilies
20 Corn husks or greaseproof paper

Instructions

1.   Cook the pork in a large pan of water with cumin, garlic and one heaped tablespoon of salt.
2.   In a separate bowl, mix the cornmeal, rest of salt and 4 cup of the beef stock until get a no sticky dough.
3.   In another bowl, cream the beef lard, toss the corn dough and mix together, taste and add salt if needed. Mix well, until you've got a thick, spoonable dough.
4.   Clean the chilies and boil them in a large pan until cook, then blend them with enough of the boiling water and salt, strain it and stew it with a tablespoon of lard.
5.   Shred the pork and toss it in the chili sauce.
6.   Take a soaked corn husk and spoon a heaped tablespoon of the corn dough into the middle of the husk; fill it with the chili beef and fold the sides in to cover the mixture. Lay your prepared tamales in a large steamer, as the indications above. Steam for about 40 to 45 minutes.

Silly Sweet Tamales

Ingredients

1 kg fine cornmeal
250 g butter
1 teaspoon baking powder
1 teaspoon vanilla extract
1 pinch salt
½ cup sugar
150 g unsweetened dried coconut
1 cup drained canned pineapple
1 cup warm water
150 g dried cranberry
Pink colorant
20 corn husks or greaseproof paper

Instructions

1.   In a bowl, mix the cornmeal, salt and 4 cups of water until get a no sticky dough.
2.   In another bowl, cream the butter and the sugar with a mixer, toss the dough, colorant and mix together.
3.   Add the diced pineapple, baking powder, vanilla, coconut and cranberry.
4.   Mix well, until you've got a thick, spoonable paste.
5.   Take a soaked corn husk and spoon a heaped tablespoon of your mixture into the middle of the husk; fold the sides in to cover the filling, then twist the ends and use husk string to tie them.
6.   Lay your prepared tamales in a large steamer, as the indications above. Steam for about 40 to 45 minutes.

**When the pork tamales are finished, the leftover corn batter is scraped out of the bowls, sweetened and used in this preparation to be not wasted.*

Sweet Corn Tamales

Ingredients

250 g fine cornmeal
2 ½ cup sweet corn
400 g butter
1 ½ tablespoon baking powder
1 teaspoon ground cinnamon
1 cup condensed milk
½ cup whole milk
20 corn husks or greaseproof paper

Instructions

1.   Blend the 200 g of sweet corn, cinnamon and the milks.
2.   Cream the butter in a different bowl and mix with the cornmeal, baking powder and the blended corn, add the rest of the sweet corn and mix again.
3.   Spoon a heaped tablespoon of the mixture into the middle of the husk; fold the sides in to cover the mixture.
4.   Steam for about 35 to 40 minutes.

Tamales Serranos

Ingredients

1 kg fine cornmeal
250 g lard
1 kg pork meat
150 g tomatoes
1 chopped green pepper bell
½ onion
½ cup cooked chickpea
¼ cup cooked peas
50 g cooked green bean
1 pinch pepper
1 pinch cumin seeds
3 garlic cloves
½ cup chopped black olives
2 bay leaf
3 heaped tablespoon salt
1 L water
1 teaspoon baking powder
20 corn husks or greaseproof paper

Instructions

1.	Boil the pork in a large pan with one garlic clove, one tablespoon of salt and a big pinch of cumin.
2.	Shred the meat, chop tomatoes, onion and garlic, then cook them with bay leaf and lard in a saucepan.
3.	In a different bowl, mix the cornmeal, rest of the salt and 4 cups of the pork stock.
4.	Also cream the lard and mix with the corn dough, baking powder, pork, beans, olives and pepper bell.
5.	Spoon a heaped tablespoon of the mixture into the middle of the husk; fold the sides in to cover the mixture.
6.	Steam for about 45 to 60 minutes.

Beverages

Ponche is the typical drink that accompanies all Christmas meals. Mexican punch is a variation of the classic English drink, substituting tea and juice for an infusion of seasonal fruits and rum or gin for tequila.

Atoles are equally popular in cold weather, and are drunk religiously as part of the offering to the Virgin of Guadalupe on December 12th and remain so until February 2nd, Candlemass Day. It is a thick drink generally prepared with corn dough and water, but it is also common to find *atoles* thickened with wheat flour, starch or other cereals and grains such as amaranth, beans or mesquite. This drink is flavored with fruit, vanilla or chocolate, but for Christmas Eve, some families prepare a complex recipe made of chocolate, cinnamon and cloves known as *puzcua* or *champurrado*.

Champurrado

Ingredients

1 L water
3 L milk
2 tablespoon cinnamon
350 g handmade chocolate
250 g piloncillo or brown sugar
400 gr cornmeal

Instructions

1.   Chop the chocolate in small pieces.
2.   Boil 1 L of milk with the cinnamon, sugar and chocolate, remove from heat when chocolate is dissolved.
3.   Toast the cornmeal in a frying pan until lightly browned, then mix with the water and set aside.
4.   Blend the rest of milk with the cornmeal mixture and the chocolate dissolved.
5.   Heat in a large pot until get thick.

Christmas Punch

Ingredients

6 apples
6 guavas
10 tejocotes (optional)
50 g raisin
50 g dried prune
5 tamarinds or 1 cup of tamarind paste
½ pineapple
2 cinnamon stick
100 gr hibiscus
10 L water
1 kg peeled cane
500 g sugar
1 L tequila

Instructions

1.   Boil the water with the cinnamon and the hibiscus. Meanwhile, chop the pineapple, apples, *tejocotes* and guavas, removing seeds and sticks.
2.   Toss the fruit, tamarind paste, cane, sugar, raisins and prunes into the water pan and keep in the fire until get an infusion of all ingredients.
3.   When serve in cups, add a dash of tequila.

Chocolate

Ingredients

2 L milk
1 L water
300 gr handmade chocolate
2 cinnamon stick
3 cloves
Sugar as needed

Instructions

1.   Boil the water with the cinnamon, sugar and the cloves.
2.   Chop the chocolate and toss it to the boiling water. Add the milk and stir constantly until chocolate is dissolves.
3.   To serve with foam, stir the chocolate with a chocolate grinder (*molinillo*) or a balloon whisk. Another way is to pour the hot chocolate into the cups using a pitcher from certain height.

Citrus Punch

Ingredients

8 yellow lemons
5 oranges
5 tangerines
4 cinnamon sticks
4 star anise
3 cloves
1 cup hibiscus
10 L water
1 kg brown sugar or piloncillo

Instructions

1.   Boil the water with the cinnamon, star anise, cloves, sugar and the hibiscus.
2.   Meanwhile, slices the fruit, then toss it into the water pot and keep in the fire until get an infusion of all ingredients.

Cookie Atole

Ingredients

3 L milk
1 L water
1 cinnamon stick
1 cup sugar
500 g vanilla cookies

Instructions

1.   Boil the milk with the cinnamon and sugar in low heat.
2.   Ground the cookies with a blender or food processor until a fine powder. Stir the ground cookies with water to dissolve.
3.   Toss the ground cookies to the milk and low heat until get thick.

Fruit Atole

Ingredients

1 L milk
½ L water
250 - 500 g local fruit
200 g sugar
60 g corn starch
1 cinnamon stick (optional)

Instructions

1.   Remove seeds from fruits and boil them with sugar over low heat.
2.   Blend them with a food processor and pour them into a large pot over low heat with 2 cups of milk.
3.   Meanwhile, dissolve the starch in the rest of milk and toss it to the pot.
4.   Stir constantly until thickened.

Wheat Atole

Ingredients

3 L water
1 L milk
2 cinnamon stick
400 g precooked wheat grain
400 g piloncillo or brown sugar
500 g cornmeal

Instructions

1.   Mix the cornmeal with the milk and 1 L water to dissolve, set aside.
2.   Boil the rest of water with the cinnamon, sugar and wheat grain.
3.   Toss the cornmeal mixture to the cinnamon water and heat until get thick.

Garnish

For the Christmas Eve dinner, most families use small versions of tamales or fried treats as sides plates. Salads are also common as a complement for main dishes such as baked turkey or roasted pork.

The mixture of lettuces and vegetables as a Christmas garnish appeared 100 years ago in Mexican cookbooks. The classic recipe is derived from the American Waldorf salad, which became famous in the early 20th century. Nowadays some versions can be found served as a dessert.

Other side dishes such as mashed potatoes can be traced back at least 200 years to Mexican tables, and although they have been simplified to a smooth purée seasoned and thickened with cheese, some families still keep sweeter and more rustic preparations.

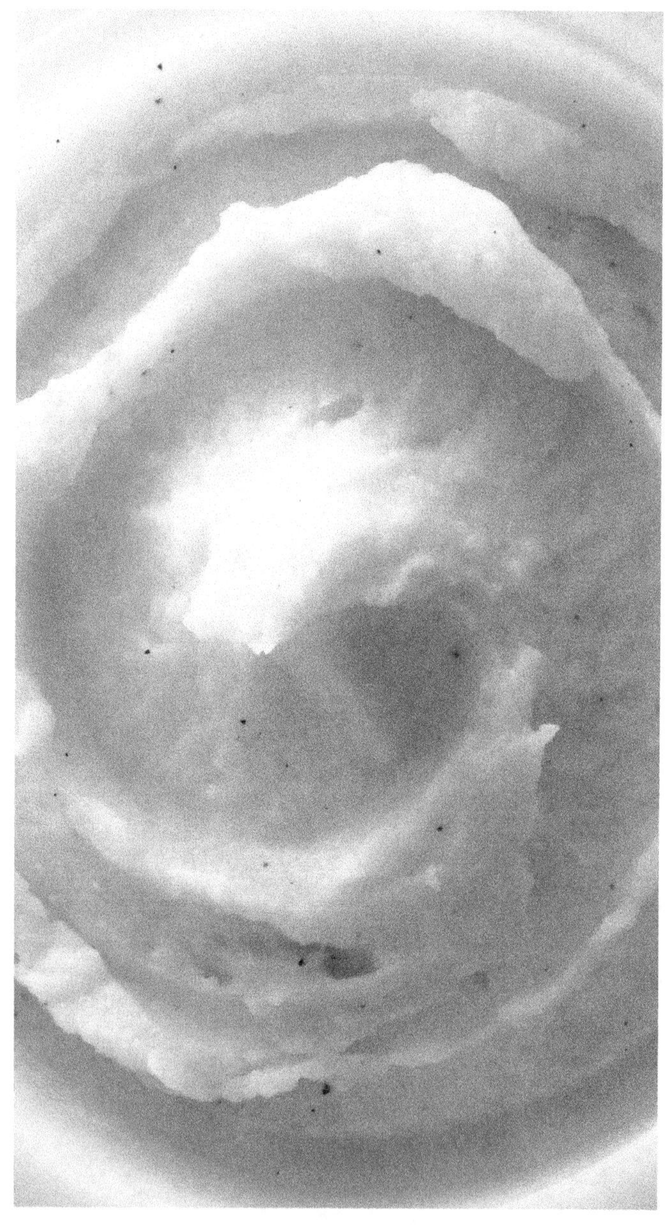

Christmas Salad

Ingredients

2 tablespoons chopped parsley
2 celery sticks
4 red apples
2 potatoes
3 carrots
100 g peas
100 g ham
1/3 cup raisins
½ sour cream
1/3 yogurt
½ pecan
2 tablespoon mayonnaise
50 g canned cherry
Sea salt

Instructions

1.   Peel and chop the carrots and the potatoes, boil them separately in salted water. Cook as well the peas in water.
2.   Chop the ham in small cubes, dice the cherry and the celery stick. Also peel the apples and diced them.
3.   Drain the cooked vegetables, then in a large bowl mix all the ingredients. Season, taste and plate.

Mashed Apple

Ingredients

1 kg potatoes
1 kg apples
1 butter
1 cup milk
100 g sugar
100 g shredded mozzarella cheese

Instructions

1.   Peel the potatoes and the apples, then chop into large chunks. Put the potatoes in a large pot of boiling salted water and boil hard for 20 minutes, or until tender.
2.   In a saucepan cook the apples with the butter, add sugar and strir until sugar is disolved
3.   Drain the potatoes and allow to steam dry, then smash them up in the pan with the milk, cheese and the cooked apple. Season with pepper.

Mashed Sweet Potato

Ingredients

1 kg potatoes
1 big sweet potato
90 g butter
½ cup milk
½ cup heavy cream
1 teaspoon black pepper

Instructions

1.	Peel the potatoes and the sweet potato, then chop into large chunks. Put them in a large pot of boiling salted water and boil hard for 20 minutes, or until tender.
2.	Drain and allow to steam dry, then smash them up in the pan with butter. For a smooth texture, add the milk and the heavy cream. Season with salt and black pepper.

Mexican Waldorf

Ingredients

200 g pecan
200 g seedless grape
3 carrots
3 apples
1 cup canned diced pineapple
2 cdas mayonnaise
1 can condensed milk
1 can evaporated milk
100 g canned cherry
2 lemon juice
1 cup tiny marshmallows

Instructions

1.   Peel the apples, then chop into small chunks. Chop the pineapple, the grapes and dice the cherries. Grate the carrot and set aside.
2.   In a large bowl, pour the milks, the mayonnaise and the juice. Toss in all the fruits, the carrots, pecan and marshmallows. Mix well and serve.

Molotes

Ingredients

1 kg corn meal
100 g rice flour
400 g mashed potatoes
1 teaspoon grounded cumin
1 teaspoon grounded black pepper
1 teaspoon grounded garlic
Chicken Stock
400 g cheese (mozzarella)

Instructions

1.	Mix the mashed potatoes with the corn meal, rice flour, spices and chicken stock needed until be a moldable dough.
2.	Heat the oil in a large saucepan.
3.	Take small portions (60 g) of the dough, fill them with cheese, shape them into an oval and fry them until rich brown.

Noche Buena Salad

Instructions

2 beets
2 oranges
2 tangerines
½ cup sugar
2 L water
1 jicama (optional)
1 cup diced pineapple
1 cup chopped pecan
1 cup peanuts
1 Romaine lettuce
100 g toasted sesame

Ingredients

1.   Top and tail the oranges and tangerines, cut away the peel, then finely slice into rounds, removing any pips.
2.   Peel and dice the beets. Cook them in water with the sugar and an orange peel until soft. Let it cool and reserve the liquids.
3.   Meanwhile, peel and dice the jicama, toast the nuts and discard the tatty outer lettuce leaves, then roughly chop.
4.   Mix together all the ingredients in a large bowl, pour in the beet liquids and let it rest 10 minutes before plating.

Mexican Christmas Main Dishes

Many of the main dishes are prepared in different celebrations throughout the year. But only a few, such as *bacalao* or *romeritos,* have managed to position themselves as Christmas Eve classics.

Towards the north of Mexico, it is common to celebrate the holidays with grilled beef meat, on the coasts with seafood and in the south with a variety of *moles*; throughout the country there is the possibility of preparing pork loins or legs larded and covered with spicy sauces; and turkeys, suckling pig or lamb stuffed with fruit and ground meat.

The variety of dishes at the dinner also depends on the local products and the possibilities of each home, but it is always a feast that is distinguished by the particular seasoning of each family.

Asado

Ingredients

1 kg chopped pork ribs
14 dried red chilies (6 ancho chilies, 4 guajillo chilies, 4 arbol chilies)
1 orange
8 garlic cloves
1 onion
100 g handmade chocolate
1 cup sugar
2 bay leafs
1 teaspoon black pepper
4 cloves
2 cinnamon stick
200 g cracker
1 Fistfull salt

Instructions

1.   Mix the pork with salt and set aside for 30 minutes.
2.   Minced 2 garlic cloves and sauté them in a saucepan with a tablespoon of lard and the ribs. Cover and simmer over low heat for 12 minutes, stirring constantly.
3.   Meanwhile, cover chilies with boiling water in a bowl. Set aside for 20 minutes to soak. Blend the chili and strain it into a bowl.
4.   Chop the onion and the rest of the garlic, then cook them in a saucepan with two tablespoons of lard. Crush the crackers and toss them into the saucepan to cook as well, adding lard as needed. Blend this mixture and set aside.
5.   In another saucepan add a tablespoon of lard, let it heat and add the chocolate, fry it for a moment, then pour into the saucepan the strained chili, the blended crackers, spices, oranges (juice and peel) and finally the ribs. Let it cook until it thickened.

Bacalao

Ingredients

1 kg dried cod
2 kg diced tomatoes
2 diced onions
1 can of red pepper bell (2 fresh red pepper bells)
2 cooked and chopped potatoes
2 tablespoon fine chopped parsley
½ cup chopped almond
5 garlic cloves
1 can pickle chili (chile güero)
200 g green olives
5 bay leaf
½ cup pickle capers
1 tablespoon salt
1 cup olive oil

Instructions

1.   Remove saltiness by soaking the cod in cold water for 48 hrs before cooking. Store it in the refrigerator and change the water each 6 hours. Drain it and set aside.
2.   In a saucepan heat the oil and cook onion until transparent, add minced garlic, diced tomatoes, chopped red pepper bell, bay leafs and season with salt. When the mixture is cooked, remove the bay leaf and blend 2 cups of this preparation and pour it back into the saucepan.
3.   Shred the cod and toss it to the tomato saucepan, mix well and add the almond, chilies, green olives, potatoes, capers and parsley.
4.   Cook for 20 minutes over low heat, taking care that it boils slightly and stirring constantly so that it doesn't stick.

Birria

Ingredients

14 garlic cloves
3 red onions
2 cup apple vinegar
4 k beef meat
1 k tomatoes
15 dried and seedless chilies
2 coriander stick
1 teaspoon grounded cumin
1 teaspoon grounded oregano
1 teaspoon grounded black pepper
4 cloves
Sal
Olive oil

Instructions

1.   Peel and chop one onion and 12 garlic cloves. Blend them with the vinegar, half of the spices and 2 tablespoons of salt. In this paste, marinate the beef meat over 30 minutes.
2.   Chop one onion, two garlic cloves and the tomatoes; cook them in a saucepan with olive oil, then blend them in a food processor.
3.   Meanwhile, cover chilies with boiling water in a bowl. Set aside for 20 minutes to soak. Blend the chili with the rest of the spices, the tomato sauce and pour into a large pot.
4.   Add the meat with the marinade and cook in low heat for 4 hours, adding the necessary water. Taste and season with salt.
5.   Finely chop the coriander and the rest of the onion and set aside
6.   Serve the *birria* sprinkled with coriander over.

Cochinita

Ingredients
1 cup bitter orange juice
1 cup apple vinegar
1 onion
12 garlic cloves
20 g cinnamon
10 g cloves
10 g allspice
20 gr bay leaf
20 g cumin
1 kg pork rib
2 kg pork chuck
200 g *achiote* or red colorant spice
500 g lard
100 ml water
Salt

Onion pickle
1 red onion
25 g oregano
½ cup white vinegar

Instructions
1.   Make a paste, bashing all the spices together with the *achiote*, vinegar and orange juice in a pestle or a blender. Marinate the pork meat overnight.
2.   Place the pork and the *adobo* in pressure cooker, add lard and close lid; bring to high pressure over high heat. Reduce heat to low and cook for 4 hours. Remove from heat. Release steam naturally. Open lid.
3.   Make a pickle chopping red onion and mixing with white vinegar, water, salt and a pinch of oregano, serve with *cochinita*.

Green Pozole

Ingredients

1 kg chicken breast
1 kg chicken drumstick
4 roasted garlic cloves
15 roasted green tomatoes
1 roasted onion
4 roasted green chilies (jalapeños)
1 teaspoon toasted cumin
1 teaspoon ground pepper
1 tablespoon lard
5 dried bay leaf
1 cup pumpkin seed
1 bunch coriander
1 tablespoon dried oregano leaves
6 radishes
1/2 lettuce
3 L water
3 ½ tablespoon salt
1.5 kg precooked pozole corn

Instructions

1.   Place the corn, water, 4 garlic cloves, bay leaf and half onion in a large pot, cook for one hour. Add the chicken and 3 tablespoons of salt and continue cooking in high heat for 1 hour. Then remove the meat, shred it and place it again in the stock.

2.   Meanwhile, with a food processor blend oregano, tomatoes, onion, garlic, chilies, pumpkin seeds, coriander, spices and ½ tablespoon salt. In a saucepan with lard fry this sauce. Cook until thickened and toss it to the chicken pot. Taste, season and plate.

3.   Chop finely the lettuce and slice the radish, place a fistful of this salad over *pozole* when served. Squeeze a lemon on it.

Mexican Turkey

Ingredients
1 x 6 kg defrosted turkey and giblets
2 garlic cloves
1/4 onion
1 pinch sea salt
1 teaspoon fine herbs

Stuffing
½ ground meat
200 g bacon
1 teaspoon ground cinnamon
1 teaspoon rosemary
4 cloves
1/4 cup sugar
1 cup white wine
1 cup diced apricot
1 cup dehydrated plum
2 cups sliced apple
200 g butter
½ cup pecan
½ almond
2 garlic cloves
1 cup chicken stock
2 dried and diced breads

Compund butter
200 g butter
60 g thyme
1 big pinch white pepper
1 teaspoon garlic powder
1 teaspoon onion powder
1 teaspoon sea salt

Instructions

1.   Preheat the oven to 220° C.

2.   Prepare the compound butter chopping the thyme and mixing with the butter, seasoning with the rest of the condiments.

3.   Push a spatula between the skin and the breast meat of the turkey to create a pocket, then push a spoon of the butter and smooth it down with the fingers. Rub any excess butter from your hands over the skin, getting into all the crannies and nooks.

4.   Cook the giblets with 2 garlic cloves, ¼ onion, 1 teaspoon fine herbs and 2 pinch of sea salt for 1 hour. Drain and chop the giblet, conserve the giblet stock.

5.   Diced the rest of the onion and the garlic, then cook them in a large saucepan with the bacon, when it gets lightly brown add the ground meat, in halfway through cooking toss in the saucepan the giblets and the rest of ingredients for stuffing, add the bread last and the reserved giblet stock with needed chicken stock to have non-dry stuffing.

6.   Fill the turkey with the stuffing and place it into a large saucepan, cover the bird with tin foil. Place the turkey in the hot oven and immediately reduce the temperature to 180° C. Cook for 25 to 30 minutes per kilo.

7.   After 30 minutes, remove the foil and spoon some fat from the bottom of the pan over the bird. Repeat this each 30 minutes. To check if it's cooked, used a thermometer, the temperature of filling has to be at least 80° C.

8.   Transfer the turkey to a platter, taking care that the liquids from the turkey remain in the pot, cover with a double layer of foil and a kitchen towel, and leave to rest for up to 2 hours.

**You can make a sauce with the remaining liquids, just add 1 tablespoon of starch and heat until thick*

Mixiotes

Ingredients

½ teaspoon cumin
½ teaspoon dried oregano leaves
½ teaspoon back pepper
½ onion
4 garlic cloves
4 chopped chicken breasts
4 chicken wings
500 g dried red chili
50 g sesame
50 g almond
50 g peanut
3 toasted bread slices
12 pieces *mixiote* or greaseproof paper
4 tablespoon lard

Instructions

1.   Soak the *mixiotes* in warm water for 20 minutes in a bowl.
2.   Fry the chilies, onion, garlic and the spices in a saucepan with the lard. Blend them in a food processor, season with salt and strain to make a paste.
3.   Toast and crush the almonds, peanuts, and sesame, reserve them.
4.   Mix the chicken with the nuts and the chili paste.
5.   Wrap a portion of chicken with a *mixiote* or with a greaseproof paper, tying a knot with the kitchen string.
6.   In a steamer, following the same steps for tamales, cook for 30-40 minutes.

Northern Barbacoa

Ingredients

1 kg beef neck bones
1 kg beef shrink
8 garlic cloves
1 sliced onion
3 red dried chilies (guajillo)
2 peeled and chopped potatoes
5 dried bay leafs
1 pinch cumin
1 tablespoon allspice blend
1 tablespoon black pepper

Instructions

1.   Make a blend, bashing all the spices together with the half of garlic and 1 tablespoon of salt in a pestle.
2.   Cover chilies with boiling water in a bowl. Set aside for 20 minutes to soak. Drain and blend the chili with the blend of spices, strain it and reserve.
3.   Place the beef in a pressure cooker with the onion and the rest of the garlic; full of water to cover all the ingredients.
4.   Cook uncovered in medium heat, when start boiling remove the foam with a strainer.
5.   Pour the chili sauce into the pot, the chopped potatoes and close the lid. Follow the instructions of the pressure cooker and cook for 45-60 minutes.
6.   Shred the meat and serve with the beef stock.

Pork Loin in Adobo

Ingredients

1 boneless pork loin
6 red dried chilies
6 garlic cloves
1 cup pineapple juice
2 tablespoon cider vinegar
2 tablespoon brown sugar
1 tablespoon fine herbs blend
1 tablespoon allspice blend
5 tomatoes
1 onion
3 tablespoon vegetable oil
Kitchen string
½ red wine bottle
3 tablespoon lard
Saucepan

Instructions

1.   Make a marinade blending wine, orange juice and 2 garlic cloves. Make some cuts on the loin and marinate with the mixture for 12 hours in a kitchen bag or a pot. Reserve the marinade, then bridle the loin with kitchen string.
2.   Cook the tomatoes, onion and 4 garlic cloves in a saucepan with oil.
3.   In enough water, boil the chilies. Blend them with the marinade and the rest of the ingredients until get a soft sauce. Strain it and set aside.
4.   Preheat the oven 160° C.
5.   In a large saucepan with lard, seal all the sides of the loin. Then rub the *adobo* sauce over the pork, cover with tin foil and cook for 45 to 60 minutes per kilo.

Red Pozole

Ingredients

40 g red chili (20 g guajillo and 20 g pasilla)
6 garlic cloves
1 teaspoon cumin
1 teaspoon pepper
1 onion
5 dried bay leaf
1 tablespoon dried oregano leaves
6 radishes
1/2 cabbage
1 kg pork rib
1 kg pork chuck
5 L water
Salt
1 K precooked *pozole* corn

Instructions

1. Place the corn, water, 4 garlic cloves, bay leaf and half onion in a large pot, cook for 90 minutes. Add the pork meat, 2 tablespoons of salt and continue cooking in high heat for 2 hours until meat and corn are tender.
2. Meanwhile, cover chilies with boiling water in a bowl. Set aside for 20 minutes to soak. Drain and process the chilies with one cup of reserved liquid, 2 garlic cloves, spices, enough salt and the rest of onion. Strain and add to the corn pot. Cook for 30 minutes. Taste, season and plate.
3. Chop finely the cabbage and slice the radish, place a fistful of this salad over pozole when served.

Romeritos with Shrimp

Ingredients
1 kg *romeritos* or spinach
1 L mole
400 g cooked and skinless potatoes
3 prickly pear or 250 gr green beans
200 g dried and skinless shrimp
100 g ground shrimp
6 eggs
1 L vegetable oil

Instructions
1.   Clean the *romeritos*, removing the soft leaves from the hard shank. If you use spinach chop them in strips. Cook them in both cases in boiling salty water.
2.   Also chop the prickly pear or the green beans in small pieces. Cook the prickly pear with the juice of a lemon in a saucepan with salted water, if you use green beans only cook them in salted water.
3.   Separate the yolks and egg whites in different bowls. With an electric hand mixer, beat the egg whites until they become stiff peaks form. Then beating them on low and add in egg yolks one at a time until they're all mixed together. Toss the ground shrimp in to the batter and mix again.
4.   Heat the oil in a deep sauce pan, then fry one tablespoon of the batter making little round shape fritters, fry them until crisp and a rich brown color, turning regularly. Drain over kitchen paper.
5.   Heat the mole in a large pan, if is necessary add a cup of chicken stock.
6.   Add into the mole the dried shrimp, fritters, prickley pear, potatoes and vegetables. Let boil once, taste, season and serve.

Traditional Mole

Ingredients

300 g dried red chili
100 g peanuts
100 g sesame
100 g pecan
100 g almond
2 small breads
½ onion
1 cinnamon stick
2 sliced bananas
1 tablespoon coriander
4 peppers
6 garlic cloves
250 g lard
100 g handmade chocolate
4 cloves
1 tablespoon anise seed
1 L chicken stock

Instructions

1.   Clean the chilies removing the seeds, then fry them quickly in a sauce pan with the lard watching not to burn, set aside.
2.   Also fry in the same lard the bananas, then the bread, onion, garlic, nuts and spices, all separately and careful not to burn it.
3.   In a large pan, heat the chocolate with a cup of chicken stock until it is dissolved.
4.   Blend all the fried ingredients with the rest of stock and water needed, strain the sauce and toss it into the large pan with the chocolate.
5.   Heat this sauce until thickened. Season with salt and sugar.

Aguinaldo

At the end of the *posadas*, children who have hit the *piñata* are given an *aguinaldo*, which in the last century was a paper bag filled with a variety of sweets, fruits and peanuts, being its predecessor in the colonial *posadas* the *calabaza en tacha*, a candy that was also given to the attendees.

A traditional *aguinaldo* contains:
1.   100 g animal cookie
2.   100 g sprinkle cookie
3.   100 g glazed cookie
4.   One piece cane stick
5.   2 oranges
6.   100 g peanuts with shell
7.   Bunch of tejocotes
8.   300 g variety hard candies

Animal Cookies

Ingredients

500 g plain flour
170 g unsalted butter
60 g sugar
1 can condensed milk
1 teaspoon baking powder
1 teaspoon vanilla extract
2 eggs

Instructions

1.   Preheat the oven to 180° C and line 2 baking sheets with baking paper or silicon mat.
2.   Place the dry ingredients into a bowl, stir.
3.   Add the rest of the ingredients and bring together to make a soft dough. Toss into the bowl flour necessary to get a non-sticky dough.
4.   Place the dough on a lightly floured work surface, and roll out to 1 cm thick. Use animal cutters to cut out shapes and place on the lined baking sheets.
5.   Bake for 12 minutes, or till the biscuits are golden brown. Let them harden and transfer them to a wire rack.

Glazed Cookies

Ingredients

1 k cookie dough
1 k caster sugar
½ cup meringue powder
½ cup water
1 lemon
Food coloring (yellow, green, pink)

Instructions

1.   Place the dough on a lightly floured work surface, and roll out to 1 cm thick. Use 3 cm diameter circular cutters to cut out shapes and place them on the lined baking sheets
2.   Bake for 12 minutes, or till the cookies are golden brown. Let them harden and transfer them to a wire rack.
3.   Place the rest of the ingredients into a bowl and, using an electric hand mixer, beat until stiff peaks form.
4.   Let the mixture stand for 10 minutes before using. Divide into 3 portions and add the coloring, one for each portion.
5.   Spoon them to cover the cookies and let them dry on a rack.

Sprinkle Cookies

Ingredients

1 k 3 cm diameter circular cookies
1 k white royal icing
1 cup color sprinkles

Instructions

1.   Pour the sprinkles on a sheet.
2.   Spoon the icing to cover the cookies, then spread the sprinkles on them to coat evenly.
3.   Let dry on a track.

Calabaza en Tacha

Ingredients

1 medium pumpkin
2 ground piloncillos or 500 g of brown sugar
2 sliced oranges
1 cinnamon stick
3 cloves
2 L milk

Instructions

1.   Chop the pumpkin into quarters with a knife.
Remove seeds.
2.   Place the pumpkin chunks in a large pot with the
pulp side up. Sprinkle over them the grounded piloncillo
and the oranges.
3.   Add 1 cup of water and cook, covered, for 40
minutes until the pumpkin softens and a dark syrup form
at the bottom.
4.   Serve in a bowl a chunk of pumpkin with syrup and
1 cup of milk.

SUBSTITUTIONS

Achiote (1 cup): Turmeric blend: 2/3 cup turmeric, 1/3 cup hibiscus powder + 1 tablespoon paprika.

Beef Lard: Pork lard or unsalted butter

Banana leaf or corn husk: greaseproof paper, grape leaf, fig leaf, oak leaf or any edible leaf.

Corn meal: for the atole you can use corn starch, potato starch, plain flour, bread crumbs, toasted pita or crushed crackers.

Guava: pear, kiwi or any citric fruit.

Handmade chocolate: Any kind of chocolate with 70% cacao at least.

Hisbicus: pomegranate juice.

Jicama: cucumber slices

Mexican chorizo (1 k): 1 k curated pork (morcilla, nduja, etc) or 1 k grounded pork + 1 spoon paprika + 1 teaspoon apple vinegar.

Mexican cream: sour cream, crème fraiche or unsweetened whipping cream

Molinillo: balloon whisk

Pecan: walnuts, almond or peanut.

Pickled chili: pickled onion or pickles.

Piloncillo: brown sugar or molasses.

Poblano chili: green pepper bell or spinach for adding green color.

Pozole corn: any kind of precooked corn or chickpeas.

Pumpkin: carrot, potato or yam.

Pumpkin seed: oilseeds as sunflower seed, sesame (tahini paste), cashew, etc.

Red dried chili (guajillo, ancho): any sweet dried chili, chili paste or paprika, just for adding red color.

Red dried chili (arbol): Chili flakes, szechuan, ají or a spicy variety.

Requesón: ricotta cheese or any creamy cheese.

Romeritos: any green chopped leaf or tender sprig, such as spinach or chard.

Sweet potato: yam or carrots.

Tamarind: mango purée.

Tejocote: Small size apples

In a *posada*, the host divides the guests into two groups, one of them will play the role of "pilgrims" outside the house, at the front door, and the other will be the "hosts", and remain inside.

The verses alternate one by one between those seeking lodging outside and those responding from behind the door.

In the 13th verse, all sing along as the "pilgrims" cross the front door.

1.   Pilgrims
In the name of heaven
we ask for lodging,
my beloved wife
cannot continue walking

2.   Hosts
This place is no inn,
stay on your trail,
I must not open,
I fear you may be a scoundrel.

3.   Pilgrims
Don't be so inhuman
and have charity too
the God of heaven
will reward you.

4.   Hosts
You may go now
and do not disturb
because if I get angry
I will beat you up.

5.   Pilgrims
We come exhaustedd
from Nazareth
I am a carpenter
by the name of Joseph.

6.   Hosts
I don't care who it is,
Please let me sleep,
I won't open for you,
it's a promise I'll keep

7.   Pilgrims
Shelter asks you
beloved housekeeper,
for just one night
the queen of heaven

8.   Hosts
Well, if she is a queen
Who solicits this on and on,
How is it that by night
She wanders all alone?

9.   Pilgrims
She is queen of heaven
My wife is Mary
and mother she will be
of the promised baby

10.   Hosts
Are you Joseph?
Is your wife Mary?
Come in, travelers,
I didn't see you clearly

11.   Pilgrims
May God repay you
for your kindness,
and may heaven shower you
with happiness

12.   Hosts
What a blessed home
that receives us with mercy
the pure virgin,
the beautiful Mary

13.   Everyone

*Welcome holy pilgrims, holy
pilgrims,
receive this humble spot
although the home is poor,
home is poor,
We offer with our hearts*

*Let us sing happily, happily
and just because
the holy family, family
Come to visit us.*

You can hear the melody
of the carol with this QR
code:

Mexican Christmas Cookbook

Book cover image and edition:
Jaime Iram Vargas Barrientos

Inside photos:
Dinner. Nicole M.
Starters. Rita E.
Pasta. A. Hassan
Fritters. Mateusz G.
Tamales. Jaime I. Vargas B.
Beverages.Aliaksandra Y.
Garnish. Anon
Main Dishes. Alpha C.
Aguinaldo. Valeria L.
Posada. Jaime I. Vargas B.